WILD WARRIORS

4 BOOKS IN 1!

BY
**JERRY
PALLOTTA**

ILLUSTRATED BY
**ROB
BOLSTER**

The publisher would like to thank the following for their kind
permission to use their photographs in the book:

Photos ©: 7 center right: Cornel Constantin/Shutterstock; 10 center: B.G. Thomson/Science Source; 19 bee:
Nagy Lehel/Shutterstock; 19 fly: annop youngrot/Shutterstock; 19 grasshopper: Geraldas Galinauskas/Shutterstock;
19 scorpion: bonzami emmanuelle/Alamy Stock Photo; 19 mosquito: KPL/Shutterstock; 19 butterfly:
AdvertisingPhotography/Alamy Stock Photo; 22 center: Genevieve Vallee/Alamy Stock Photo; 23 top: Dr
Morley Read/Science Source; 23 bottom: Mehmet Karatay/Wikipedia; 24 top: Natursports/Shutterstock; 25 top:
Henri Koskinen/Alamy Stock Photo; 36: anankkml/Getty Images; 37: Eric Isselee/Shutterstock; 38 bottom:
reisegraf.ch/Shutterstock; 48 bottom: fabio fersa/Shutterstock; 52 top: Jami Tarris/Getty Images; 53 bottom:
Courtesy Skunk Works® Lockheed Martin Corporation; 56 center: Julesuyttenbroeck/Dreamstime; 59 top:
Panoramic Images/Alamy Stock Photo; 75 top right: flySnow/Getty Images; 75 bottom right: Pigprox/Shutterstock;
79 crab pot: NOAA Central Library Historical Fisheries Collection; 82 top: Carol Perry Davis; 82 bottom: Dorset
Media Service/Alamy Stock Photo; 83 bottom: Shari Romar; 87 top: Millard H. Sharp/Science Source; 96 top:
IanCale/Getty Images; 96 center top: dfikar/Fotolia; 96 center bottom: Claire Fulton/Dreamstime; 96 bottom:
lucaar/Fotolia; 97 top: 7activestudio/Fotolia; 97 center top: Mike Neale/Dreamstime; 97 center bottom:
betweenthelines/Fotolia; 97 bottom: gregg williams/Fotolia; 98: Audrey Snider-Bell/Shutterstock; 104: Courtesy
Kyle Shepherd/Louisville Zoo; 105: Dan Porges; 110: John Cancalosi/Media Bakery; 111: Panoramic Images/
Alamy Stock Photo; 112 center: Don Juan Moore/AP Images; 113 bottom left: Robert Paul Laschon/
Shutterstock; 113 bottom right: Robert Paul Laschon/Shutterstock.

Welcome to the earth, Lucian Smith Robinson!
Thank you to Barbara Burns and all my pals at Norfolk Academy.
To Bob, Betsy, and especially Christopher Detwiler.
To Grace Stevenson, who loves to read!
                                            —J.P.

To Ant Barbara, Ant Elaine, Ant Pattie, Ant Peg, Ant Sue, and Ant Val.
Dedicated to all who make their living on the ocean.
To Charlie, Eddie, Bobby D., and Teddy.
To Charlie, Eddie, Bobby D., and Ted, who love to learn!
                                            —R.B.

ISBN 978-1-339-01106-6

10 9 8 7 6 5 4 3 2 1   23 24 25 26 27

Printed in China   38
This edition first printing, 2023

Cover design by Marissa Asuncion

-TABLE of CONTENTS-

What would happen if green ants had a war against army ants? Who do you think would win?

MEET A GREEN ANT

Scientific name: *Oecophylla smaragdina*. Ants are insects that have a three-section body: head, thorax, and abdomen. The legs of an ant come out of its thorax. Insects have six legs.

abdomen

thorax

head

BODY FACT
Ants have a thin waist.

WIDE-AWAKE FACT
Ants never sleep.

DID YOU KNOW?
Green ants are also called weaver ants or green tree ants.

Green ants live in **Australia**.

World Map

MEET AN ARMY ANT

Scientific name: *Eciton burchelli*. In Africa, army ants are also called *marabunta*.

head

abdomen

thorax

OUCH FACT
An army ant has a stinger at the end of its abdomen.

Most ants and other insects have compound eyes. Army ants have two eyes and are mostly blind.

DEFINITION
A compound eye has hundreds of tiny individual eyes in one.

compound eye close-up

Most army ants live in **South America** and **Africa**.

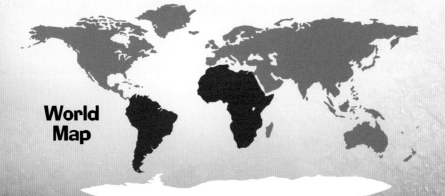

World Map

COLONY

Most green ants live in colonies of about a half million ants.

DEFINITION
An ant colony is a group of ants living and working together.

MATH FACT
A half million equals 500,000 ants.

FACT
A colony could be as few as 20 ants or up to many thousands of ants.

LEGION

Army ants live in a legion of between a half million and a million individual ants.

POPULATION FACT
Scientists once discovered a legion of about 20 million army ants.

DEFINITION
Legion means an army or large number.

NUMBER FACT
A million looks like this: 1,000,000. It means a thousand thousands.

NAME FACT
Army ants got their name because they act like a well-trained army.

Ants have been on Earth for more than 100 million years. Ants were around when dinosaurs walked on Earth. Some ants may have had fights with dinosaurs.

TREES

Green ants live in trees. Why live on the ground when you can live more safely in a tree?

DOWN-TO-EARTH FACT
Except for green ants, almost all other ant species live on the ground.

DID YOU KNOW?
Every ant has a job—some ants cut, other ants hold, and other ants glue.

Green ants weave homes made of leaves. One of the largest green-ant colonies ever seen was spread over 12 trees. Green ants usually stay in one place.

FUN FACT
Green ants use the fluid from their larvae as glue.

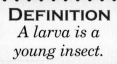
ANT LARVAE

DEFINITION
A larva is a young insect.

GROUND

Army ants live on the ground. They do not build permanent places to live. Army ants are often on the move. About every two weeks, they bivouac to another location.

DID YOU KNOW?
A bivouac is a temporary camp.

12 weeks ago

10 weeks ago

8 weeks ago

6 weeks ago

4 weeks ago

FACT
Army ants are nomads.

now

2 weeks ago

MOVEMENT FACT
When ants move, they march in a fan-shaped swarm.

DEFINITION
A nomad lives in more than one place.

DIFFERENT ANTS

There are more than 10,000 different types of ants. We could have matched up many other kinds in this book.

TURTLE ANT

DINOSAUR ANT

LEAF-CUTTER ANT

THIEF ANT

TRAP-JAW ANT

HEARING FACT
Ants do not have ears. They hear through their feet, which pick up vibrations.

BREATHING FACT
Ants do not have lungs. They get oxygen from holes in their bodies called spiracles.

ANT SPIRACLE
extreme close-up

MORE ANTS

Ants are tiny, but they come in all shapes and sizes.

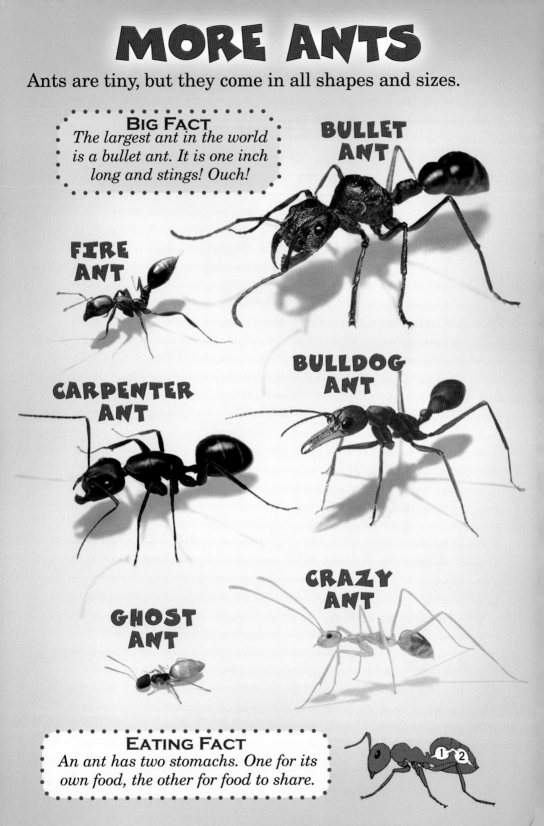

BIG FACT
The largest ant in the world is a bullet ant. It is one inch long and stings! Ouch!

BULLET ANT

FIRE ANT

CARPENTER ANT

BULLDOG ANT

CRAZY ANT

GHOST ANT

EATING FACT
An ant has two stomachs. One for its own food, the other for food to share.

SOCIETY

Every ant in the green-ant colony has a job to do. Their slogan might be: *Do your job!* Every green ant is like an engineer ready to build a nest or help its colony.

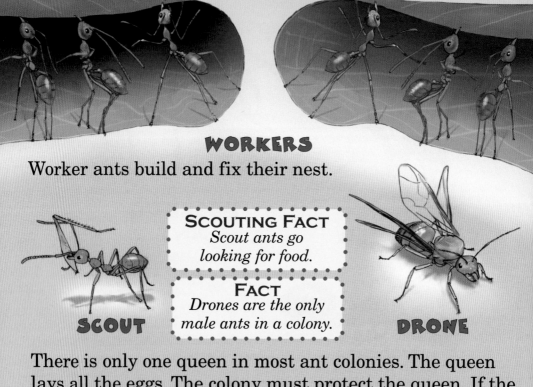

WORKERS

Worker ants build and fix their nest.

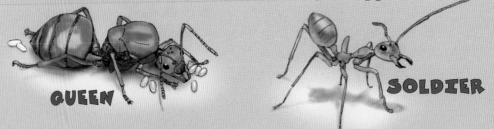

SCOUTING FACT
Scout ants go looking for food.

FACT
Drones are the only male ants in a colony.

SCOUT

DRONE

There is only one queen in most ant colonies. The queen lays all the eggs. The colony must protect the queen. If the queen dies, the colony will eventually disappear.

QUEEN

SOLDIER

Soldier ants protect the nest. They fight enemy ants.

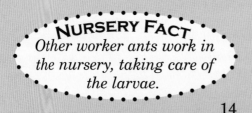

NURSERY FACT
Other worker ants work in the nursery, taking care of the larvae.

FAMILY STRUCTURE

A common human family has a mom, a dad, and a few kids. The average army-ant family has 1 mom (the queen), 20 dads (winged drones), 20 potential new moms (winged princesses), and 500,000 to 1,000,000 kids (worker ants and soldier ants).

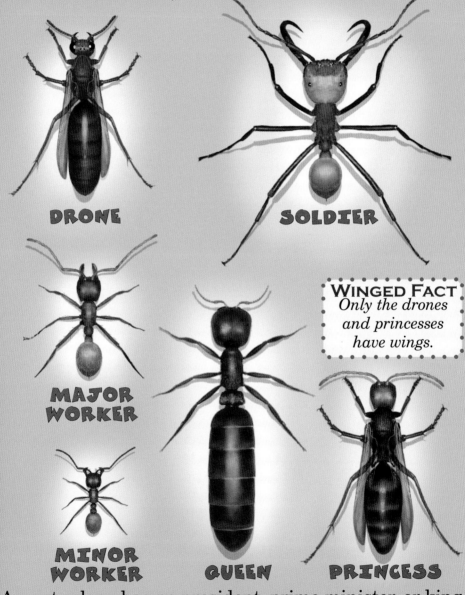

DRONE

SOLDIER

MAJOR WORKER

WINGED FACT
Only the drones and princesses have wings.

MINOR WORKER

QUEEN

PRINCESS

An ant colony has no president, prime minister, or king. But there is a queen. An ant colony thinks together as one unit.

MANDIBLES

An ant's major weapon is its mandibles.

DEFINITION
*Mandibles are part of
an animal's jaw.*

MANDIBLES

These are the mandibles of a green ant. The mandibles
have moving parts that can bite, pick up, and hold food.

JAWS

The pincers of ants are also called its jaws. This is the jaw of a soldier army ant.

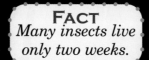

FACT
Many insects live only two weeks.

AGE FACT
Ants are among the longest living of all insects.

DID YOU KNOW?
Some queen ants have lived up to 30 years.

If you were an ant, which jaw would you rather have?

BITE

There are several types of ant jaws.

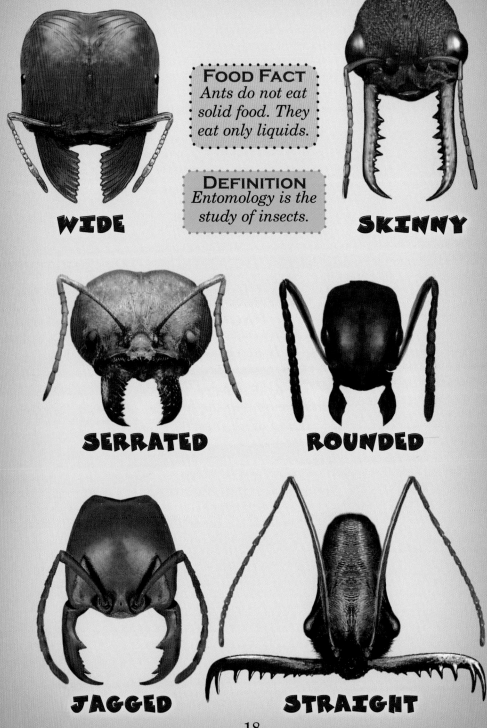

FOOD FACT
Ants do not eat solid food. They eat only liquids.

DEFINITION
Entomology is the study of insects.

WIDE

SKINNY

SERRATED

ROUNDED

JAGGED

STRAIGHT

SIP, CHEW

You can often tell how a bug eats or behaves by its mouth parts.

A **BEE** is a licker. It would enjoy an ice-cream cone just like you might.

A **FLY** is a sponger. When it lands, it "sponges" back and forth looking for food.

A **GRASSHOPPER** is a chewer. Its mouth is shaped to chew grass and leaves.

A **SCORPION** is a pincher. It has no teeth. Its mouth has pincers inside.

A **MOSQUITO** is a bloodsucker. It stabs with its needle-shaped face.

A **BUTTERFLY** is a sipper. It uses its curly tube-shaped proboscis like a straw.

Is a **DARWIN BEETLE** a clipper? No! It uses its long jaws to flip and throw other insects.

STRONG

Ants can lift things that are much heavier than they are. They can raise between 20 and 50 times their own weights.

SPEED FACT
Most ants travel less than 1 mile per hour.

SPEED FACT
Green ants walk a little slower than army ants.

If you were an ant, you could lift . . .

 a car,

DEFINITION
Myrmecology is the scientific study of ants.

or a pickup truck,

 or maybe an elephant.

WEIGHT LIFTERS

Here is a leaf-cutter ant raising a huge chunk of a leaf.

This is a dinosaur ant picking up a stone.

Here is a bulldog ant lifting its precious larvae.

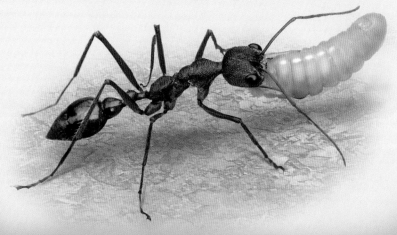

GREATEST WEAPON

The green ants' greatest weapon is their numbers. The ants warn one another of danger by releasing a chemical called a pheromone.

Thousands of ants are called to battle to protect their colony. Ants bite their enemies to death.

Another important weapon is how well organized green ants are. They work together to build an ant bridge across a gap.

GO GREEN
Green ants are camouflaged. They hide more easily in green leaves.

WEAPON

The army ants' greatest weapon is also their huge numbers. Any animal can fight against one ant. But can you fight a million ants?

GROUNDED FACT
Army ants are also camouflaged. They are brown and black. Army ants blend in against the dark ground and dead leaves they walk on.

DEFINITION
Zoology is the study of animals.

"FARMER" ANTS

Leaf-cutter ants are like farmers. They grow their own food. These ants make piles of insect and leaf parts and grow fungus. They eat the fungus.

"STORAGE" ANTS

Honeypot ants store honey in their abdomens so the colony will have food.

FACT
Ants are so organized that scientists use them as models of human behavior.

"COWBOY" ANTS

Herder ants "herd cattle." They capture aphids, a small insect, and corral, or keep them for future meals. The ants eat a liquid produced by the aphids.

"LANDSCAPER" ANTS

Some ants are landscapers. They prune and weed around their colony. Any paths that enemies could use to attack the colony are cut back.

WORD GAME!

Can you solve these word puzzles? Each answer uses **ANT** and a few other letters. We've filled in a few letters—and the first answer—to get you started!

KEY = **ANT**

P **S** =

= **R**

H __ __ __ =

= __ __ __ __ __ __

L __ __ __ =

Find the answers on page 33.

At the trunk of a tree, a few army ants attack some wandering green ants. The green ants spray formic acid into the air.

The formic acid alerts other green ants nearby to join the fight. They drop what they are doing and head to battle. The spray irritates the army ants' eyes and makes it hard for them to breathe.

Uh-oh! It's a full battle. Thousands of green ants are fighting thousands of army ants.

The green ants try to trick the army ants. The green ants are clever. They divert the fight away from their queen. If she is saved, the colony can live on.

The army ants have greater numbers and start winning the battle.

The army ants advance in an overwhelming force.
Ants, ants, and more army ants.

The green ants retreat. They realize they can't win the massive battle they began. The war is no fun.

The army ants win! There are many dead green ants to eat. The army ants have a feast. The surviving green ants return to their queen. Tomorrow they will rebuild their colony.

Puzzle answers: pants, antler, hydrant, elephant, lantern, mantis, antelope, antenna, Antarctica, eggplant

What would happen if a skunk and a jaguar came nose to nose? If they had a fight, who do you think would win?

MEET THE JAGUAR

The jaguar is a mammal in the cat family. It is the third-largest cat on Earth. The jaguar is a skilled hunter and an excellent swimmer. Its scientific name is *Panthera onca*.

DEFINITION
A mammal is a warm-blooded animal that often has hair or fur.

BIG FACT
The Siberian tiger is the largest of all cats.

SECOND FACT
The lion is the second-largest cat.

MEET THE SKUNK

The skunk is a mammal in the Mephitidae family. A striped skunk's scientific name is *Mephitis mephitis*, which means "bad smell." Skunks have black-and-white fur.

FACT
The word "skunk" comes from the Algonquin language.

The skunk is not known for its scary teeth or sharp claws. It is famous because it can make a stink!

CLIMB

Jaguars can climb trees. They often drag their freshly killed prey up into the branches of a tree.

SWIM

Most cats do not like to go in the water, but the jaguar is an excellent swimmer. Watch out, crocodiles! Watch out, turtles!

HIDE

The skunk is good at hiding. It is rarely seen during daylight. Where is the skunk?

NOISY FACT
If you hear an animal on your roof, it's probably a raccoon or a squirrel, not a skunk.

QUESTION
Have you ever smelled a skunk in your neighborhood?

Under the house? In the trash can? Over there by the bushes?

KNOW YOUR CAT FUR

jaguar:
rosettes

leopard:
c-shaped spots

cheetah:
polka dots

tiger:
stripes

lion:
plain

KNOW YOUR STRIPES

zorilla

hog-nosed
skunk

spotted
skunk

hooded
skunk

FURRY FACT
*Baby skunks are born
with stripes.*

striped
skunk

This is a stinky page! In this book we will feature the
striped skunk.

The jaguar lives in much of Central America and South America.

PACIFIC OCEAN

NORTH AMERICA

ATLANTIC OCEAN

CENTRAL AMERICA

SOUTH AMERICA

jaguar territory

FACT
Jaguars do not live in Africa.

Many jaguars live in rain forests. They also hunt on grassland and savannas.

WORLD

Skunks are found on every continent except Antarctica and Australia.

ARCTIC OCEAN

EUROPE

ASIA

PACIFIC OCEAN

AFRICA

INDIAN OCEAN

skunk territory

AUSTRALIA

SOUTHERN OCEAN

ANTARCTICA

CREPUSCULAR

The jaguar sometimes is a crepuscular hunter.

DEFINITION
"Crepuscular" means an animal hunts at dawn and at dusk.

AUTO FACT
There is a famous sports car called the Jaguar.

Dawn is when the sun first rises. Dusk is when the sun sets.

TIME-OF-DAY FACTS
Dawn is also called daybreak.
Dusk is also called twilight.

NOCTURNAL

The skunk is a nocturnal hunter. It comes out at night.

"Hey, Rob, maybe we should write a nocturnal alphabet book." —Jerry

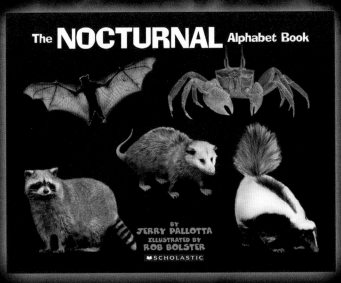

The **NOCTURNAL** Alphabet Book

BY
JERRY PALLOTTA
ILLUSTRATED BY
ROB BOLSTER
■SCHOLASTIC

DINNER

Zoologists studied jaguars and discovered that they eat dozens of different types of animals.

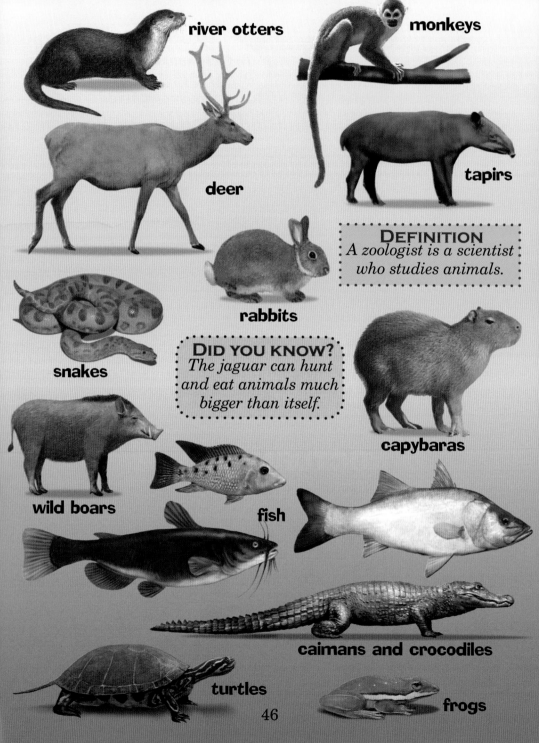

river otters

monkeys

deer

tapirs

DEFINITION
A zoologist is a scientist who studies animals.

rabbits

DID YOU KNOW?
The jaguar can hunt and eat animals much bigger than itself.

snakes

capybaras

wild boars

fish

caimans and crocodiles

turtles

frogs

46

SUPPER

Skunks are omnivores. They eat plants and animals. A skunk would gladly eat spaghetti or a cheeseburger, too.

fruits and vegetables

insects and larvae

small reptiles and amphibians

small mammals

eggs

fish

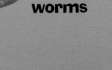

worms

snails

spaghetti

cheeseburger

47

WARNING
BEWARE THE JAGUAR

The jaguar is a magnificent creature. If there were an animal Olympics, the jaguar might win the gold medal for hunting.

However, the jaguar is not a gentle animal. It stalks and ambushes its prey. Its jaws are so strong it can bite turtle shells, pierce skulls, and crush necks.

TAIL FACT
The jaguar has the shortest tail of all the big cats; the snow leopard has the longest tail.

WARNING BEWARE THE SKUNK

One day, a skunk sprayed the underside of a car. The car smelled so bad the family couldn't drive it for a week. Stinky!

A skunk was near a home's outdoor air-conditioning unit. The skunk got startled and sprayed. The smell went through the central air vents in the house, and the people couldn't live there for a month. It wasn't funny!

A girl got sprayed by a skunk on her way to school. The principal sent her home. To get the skunk smell off, she had to take a bath in tomato juice. Her parents had to throw her clothes away.

HEAR

How might you know a jaguar is in the area? You would hear it! The jaguar is the only cat in the Western Hemisphere that roars.

> **MEOW FACT**
> *House cats meow.*
> *Lions, tigers, leopards,*
> *and jaguars roar!*

SMELL

How would you know a skunk is in the area? You might smell it! Yuck! The skunk's smell comes from glands near its tail. The skunk lifts its tail and shoots its stinky mist.

FACT

Skunks are less likely to spray if they can't see what they are spraying. If a pest-removal worker catches a skunk in a cage, he might cover the cage with a blanket so the skunk won't spray.

ALONE

The jaguar is a solitary cat. It is perfectly happy living alone.

DEFINITION
"Solitary" and "solo" both mean "alone."

This might be what it would look like if jaguars hunted in a pack. Yikes!

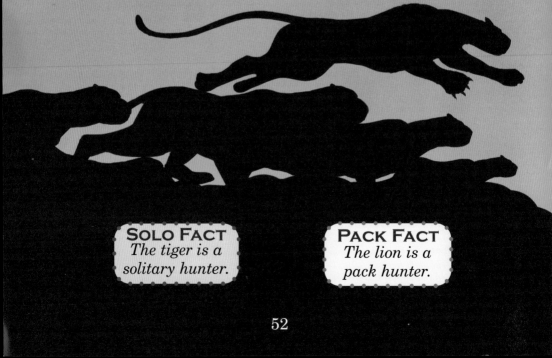

SOLO FACT
The tiger is a solitary hunter.

PACK FACT
The lion is a pack hunter.

COOL SMELLY FACTS

The name "Chicago" is from the Ojibwa language for "skunk land."

CHICAGO SKYLINE

DID YOU KNOW?
Skunk cabbage smells like skunk spray.

Skunk Works® was the secret name of the Lockheed Martin aircraft factory in Palmdale, California, which built the top secret U-2 spy plane, the SR-71 Blackbird, the F-117 Nighthawk stealth fighter, and the F-22 Raptor.

The jaguar has teeth that are perfect for catching and eating meat.

HEIGHT AND WEIGHT

36 INCHES

26"–30" HIGH AT SHOULDER

24

WEIGHT
120–210 pounds

12

0

LENGTH AND WEIGHT

INCHES

0   12   24   36

22"–31" LONG

WEIGHT
4–12
pounds

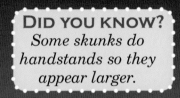

MORE WEAPONS

The jaguar has other weapons besides its huge teeth and strong jaws.

SHARP CLAWS

CAMOUFLAGE

SPEED/QUICKNESS

Wow! A jaguar can run fifty miles per hour. That is really moving!

ONE WEAPON

Maybe all you need is one secret weapon. The skunk's ability to create a terrible smell has kept it safe for millions of years.

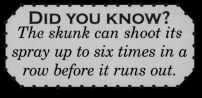

DID YOU KNOW?
The skunk can shoot its spray up to six times in a row before it runs out.

FACT
Skunk spray is highly flammable.

STINK

20 mph

10 mph

Skunks aren't fast. But they are experts in chemical warfare.

The jaguar sneaks up on a napping crocodile and crushes its neck with one giant bite!

As the jaguar was eating the crocodile, the skunk found a tasty dragonfly.

I wish I was a human. I'd have a pepperoni pizza, a cheeseburger, and fries.

As the jaguar was eating a nutria, the skunk was munching on a delicious frog.

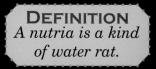

DEFINITION
A nutria is a kind of water rat.

The jaguar ambushes a capybara, the largest rodent on Earth. It hauls the big rodent up its tree to save for a dinner later.

A big green anaconda for lunch also is no problem. The jaguar's jaws are strong! Sorry, snake!

The jaguar catches a giant pacu with its pointy teeth. Yum! It will have fish for dinner tonight.

As the jaguar was eating the giant pacu, the skunk chewed and swallowed a turtle egg.

FACT
A skunk was seen chasing a cougar away.

The jaguar's jaw is so strong it can pierce a tough turtle shell. The jaguar will eat the turtle.

The smart jaguar stalks a wild boar. It patiently waits for the boar to go to sleep, then crushes its skull.

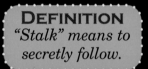

DEFINITION
"Stalk" means to secretly follow.

The hungry jaguar is walking in the rain forest. It is looking for another meal.

The jaguar sees the skunk. The jaguar could easily rip the skunk to shreds. This may be no contest.

The jaguar can't stand the smell. It runs away as fast as possible. Congratulations to the skunk. The ferocious jaguar quit the battle. STINK WINS!

WHO WOULD WIN?

LOBSTER VS. CRAB

What if a lobster and a crab bumped into each other. What if they had a fight? Who do you think would win?

WHICH LOBSTER?

Which lobster should fight the crab?

SPINY LOBSTER

Spiny lobster from the Caribbean? Sorry, you are spiky, but have no claws.

PINK SPOTTED PRAWN

Pink spotted prawn? No way! You are a shrimp, not a lobster.

Shovel-nosed lobster? Nope, you are strange looking. Go dig up a clam!

SHOVEL-NOSED LOBSTER

American lobster? Perfect! Two claws.

AMERICAN LOBSTER

WHICH CRAB?

Which crab should fight the lobster?

DUNGENESS CRAB

Dungeness crab? No! It is famous in San Francisco and on the West Coast. Its shell is rubbery.

ALASKAN KING CRAB

Alaskan king crab? No! You have only six legs. You are popular in restaurants all over the world.

FACT
Crabs have eight legs and two claws.

HORSESHOE CRAB

Horseshoe crab? No! You are not even a crab. You look prehistoric!

BLUE CRAB

Blue crab? Yes, you are one of the best-known crabs in the world. And maybe the best tasting.

MEET THE LOBSTER

The American lobster's scientific name is *Homarus americanus*. It lives off America's northeast and Canada's east coasts.

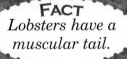

FACT
Lobsters have a muscular tail.

FACT
Lobsters are in an animal family called crustaceans.

WILD FACT
A lobster's teeth are in its stomach.

The largest lobster was about three feet long and weighed 44 pounds.

MEET THE BLUE CRAB

This is a blue crab. It is the most popular crab in the world. Its scientific name is *Callinectes sapidus,* which means "beautiful savory swimmer."

DEFINITION
Savory means pleasant or agreeable in taste or smell.

BITE FACT
A blue crab can't bite with its mouth. A grinding mill inside its body chews its food.

DID YOU KNOW?
Blue crabs are known as "swimming crabs."

DID YOU KNOW?
A blue crab does not have a tail.

The largest blue crab was about one foot wide and weighed a little more than one pound.

WHERE DO LOBSTERS LIVE?

American lobsters live from North Carolina's coastline up to Canada's east coast. Lobsters can be found in shallow water close to shore and also in deep water miles out.

CANADA

UNITED STATES

Range of the American lobster

WHERE DO CRABS LIVE?

Blue crabs are most often found from the south shore of Cape Cod in Massachusetts all the way down to the Texas-Mexico border. Chesapeake Bay is one of the most famous places for blue crabs.

FACT
Chesapeake Bay is an estuary. An estuary is where the ocean meets a river.

U.S.A.

Range of the blue crab in the U.S.

BONUS FACT
More than 150 rivers and streams empty into the Chesapeake Bay.

DID YOU KNOW?
Blue crabs love shallow, brackish water.

DEFINITION
Brackish water is part salt and part freshwater.

MEXICO

71

LOBSTER PARTS

The lobster's head and thorax is one piece. It's called a *cephalothorax*. A lobster has eight legs, just like a spider and a scorpion.

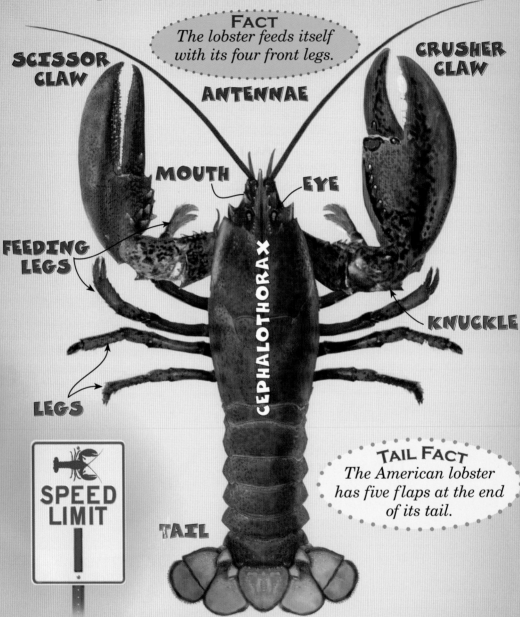

SCISSOR CLAW

FACT
The lobster feeds itself with its four front legs.

ANTENNAE

CRUSHER CLAW

MOUTH

EYE

FEEDING LEGS

CEPHALOTHORAX

KNUCKLE

LEGS

SPEED LIMIT

TAIL FACT
The American lobster has five flaps at the end of its tail.

TAIL

On land, lobsters cannot walk well. The front two legs on each side have pincers on them.

CRAB ANATOMY

The blue crab's body is one piece. Its shell is called a *carapace*.

RUNNING FACT
A blue crab walks and runs sideways.

WALKING FACT
A soldier crab is one of the few crabs that walks forward.

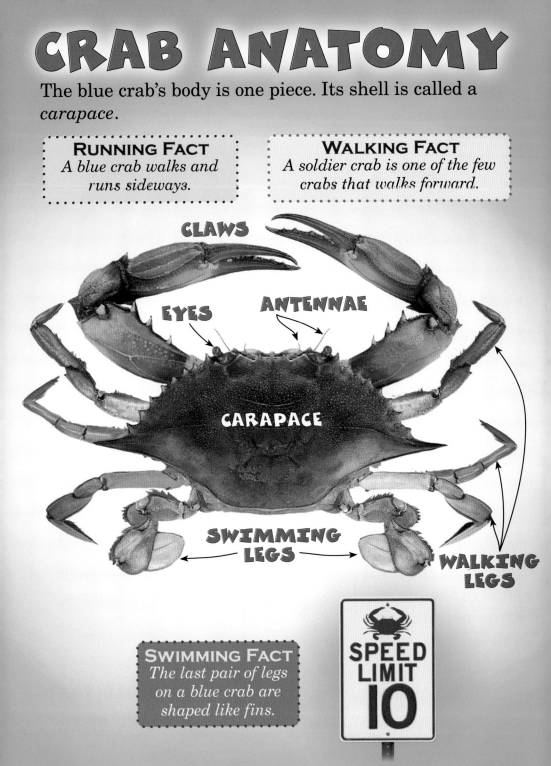

CLAWS

EYES

ANTENNAE

CARAPACE

SWIMMING LEGS

WALKING LEGS

SWIMMING FACT
The last pair of legs on a blue crab are shaped like fins.

SPEED LIMIT 10

Blue crabs can swim well, and they're also great runners. They can run fast on land.

73

BOY

The crusher claw of a male lobster is bigger and wider than a female crusher claw. The flaps under the tail are called swimmerettes.

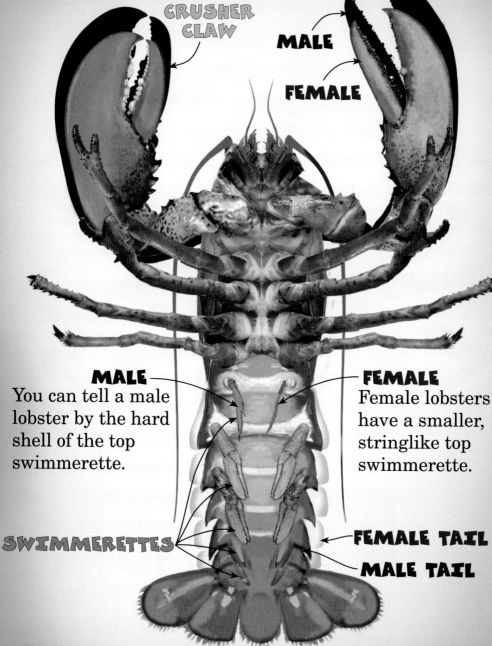

CRUSHER CLAW

MALE

FEMALE

MALE
You can tell a male lobster by the hard shell of the top swimmerette.

FEMALE
Female lobsters have a smaller, stringlike top swimmerette.

SWIMMERETTES

FEMALE TAIL

MALE TAIL

Female lobster tails are wider than male lobster tails.

OR GIRL!

Crabs have a flap between their eight legs that is called an apron or a leaf. The girls' leaf is shaped like the Capitol Dome. Girl blue crabs also have red tips on their claws. They look like painted fingernails.

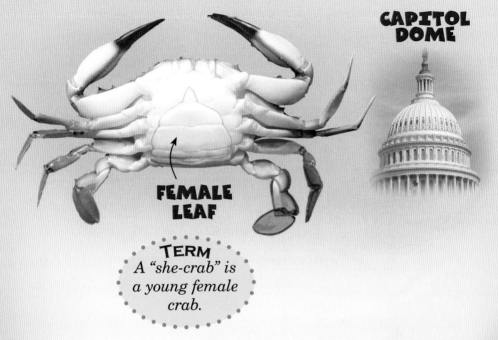

CAPITOL DOME

FEMALE LEAF

TERM
A "she-crab" is a young female crab.

Boy blue crabs have a skinny leaf. Some say it is shaped like the Washington Monument.

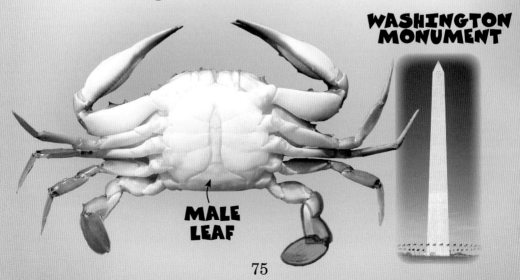

WASHINGTON MONUMENT

MALE LEAF

LOBSTER CLAWS

The two claws of a lobster are different. The crusher claw is dull and the scissor claw is sharp.

CRUSHER CLAW

The crusher claw is slower and stronger, and usually wider. The scissor claw is quicker and skinnier.

> **DID YOU KNOW?**
> *Some kids call them a cruncher claw and a ripper claw. Other kids call them a smasher claw and a slasher claw.*

SCISSOR CLAW

Either claw could be on the right or the left.

CRAB PINCERS

Can you call them claws or pincers?
Both words are correct.

CLAW TYPE
*Blue crab claws are
not specialized.*

FACT
*The claws of a blue crab are similar. Each claw
is a mirror image of the other claw.*

QUESTION?
*Is this blue crab
male or female?*

ANSWER
*The clues you'll need
are on page 75.*

LOBSTER BAIT

Most lobsters are caught by traps. Traps are baited with fish heads, fish guts, and fish bones.

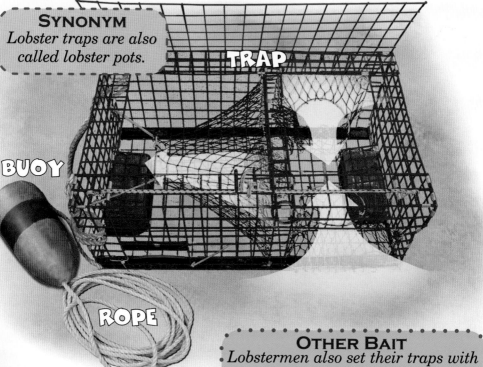

SYNONYM
Lobster traps are also called lobster pots.

TRAP

BUOY

ROPE

OTHER BAIT
Lobstermen also set their traps with deer hides, hot dogs, chicken necks, steak bones, and even roadkill!

BUOY COLOR?

A buoy is a marker that floats on top of the water. Lobstermen can tell their gear by the colors of the buoy.

QUESTION?
If you were a lobsterman or lobsterwoman, what colors would your buoy be?

CATCH A CRAB

Blue crabs are caught by crab pots, trotlines, and by a dip net.

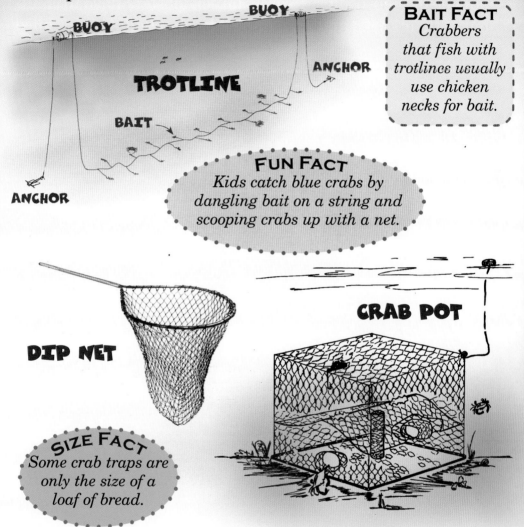

BUOY

BUOY

ANCHOR

TROTLINE

BAIT

ANCHOR

BAIT FACT
Crabbers that fish with trotlines usually use chicken necks for bait.

FUN FACT
Kids catch blue crabs by dangling bait on a string and scooping crabs up with a net.

DIP NET

CRAB POT

SIZE FACT
Some crab traps are only the size of a loaf of bread.

Crabs love fresh bait. Chicken, fish, steak, or any meat works well.

CHICKEN

FISH

STEAK

EXOSKELETON

Lobsters have an exoskeleton, which is a hard shell on the outside of their bodies. To grow larger, lobsters have to climb out of their shells and then grow a larger shell. This is called molting.

■ OLD EXOSKELETON

■ MOLTING SOFT SHELL LOBSTER

HARDSHELL
A lobster with a hard shell.

FACT
The younger a lobster is, the more it molts.

GROSS FACT
After molting, a lobster eats its old shell.

SOFT SHELL
A recently molted lobster whose shell is delicate.

80

MOLTING

Crabs also have an exoskeleton and molt to grow larger.

DID YOU KNOW?
A "peeler" is a crab about to shed its shell.

DEFINITION
A "hardshell" is a crab that is not molting and has a hard shell.

OLD EXOSKELETON

MOLTING SOFT SHELL CRAB

SOFT FACT
A "soft shell" is a crab that has just shed its shell.

FACT
A crustacean that molts is vulnerable to predators while in a soft state.

EGGER

A female lobster with eggs is called an egger or a seeder. She carries the eggs, which are dark green, under her tail attached to her body and swimmerettes.

DID YOU KNOW?
Out of 50,000 eggs, it is estimated that only two grow up to be as large as their mother.

The eggs turn light orange and hatch. The mom lobster carries between 3,000 and 75,000 eggs.

TASTY FACT
One day after hatching, about half the eggs get eaten by fish and other predators.

BABY LOBSTER

SPONGER

A sponger is a female crab with eggs. The crab below is a female blue crab whose leaf is full of eggs.

EGGS

Scientists think there are up to two million eggs in a large blue crab.

BABY BLUE CRAB

LOBSTER EYES

Lobsters can't see well. They have antennae that sense vibrations in the water. They have a great sense of smell.

LOBSTER TERMS

KEEPER
A lobster large enough to legally keep.

V-NOTCH TAIL
A female lobster that has been notched by the Department of Fisheries cannot be kept.

CHICKEN LOBSTER
A keeper lobster that weighs under 1 pound.

CULL
A lobster with only one claw.

CRAB EYES

Crabs can't see well. They have a great sense of smell and their antennae can sense motion.

CRAB VOCABULARY

SOOK
A mature female blue crab.

JIMMY
A male blue crab.

WEAPONS

Lobsters have spikes all over their shells. They are armored and ready for battle.

Spikes on the nose.

Spikes on the tail.

Spikes on the knuckles.

FACT
A lobster can curl its tail and cut your fingers or hand.

DEFENSIVE FACT
Lobsters use their claws to defend themselves against fish and other creatures.

MEASURING

QUESTION?
How do you measure a lobster?

ANSWER
With a lobster gauge.

Measure from the eye socket to the end of its head. In most states, the head must be 3-¼ inches long to be a keeper.

ARMOR

A crab has sharp points around its body. Take a good look at a blue crab. Predators can't easily swallow it.

GAUGE

QUESTION?
How do you measure a blue crab?

ANSWER
With a crab gauge.

Measure a crab from point to point, from side to side. In most states, a crab must be at least five inches long to be a keeper.

ARE YOU HUNGRY?

Someone once said, "Everything tastes like chicken, but nothing tastes as good as lobster."

EAT BEFORE THE FIGHT

Other people say blue crab is the greatest food on earth.

The lobster wants to be left alone. It climbs into a crevice. The crab wants to be left alone, too. It burrows into some mud.

They both get hungry. The crab walks around, looking for food. It stumbles upon the lobster. The crab tries to take a bite.

Whoosh! The lobster flaps its tail and gets away. The crab runs after it. Whoosh! Another flap of its tail, and the lobster gets away. But the lobster is hungry. It walks claws-first at the crab.

The crab flaps its paddle-shaped legs and swims over to the lobster. The lobster is patient. When the crab gets close, the lobster attacks.

The lobster's quick scissor claw grabs the crab by one of its claws. The lobster's crusher claw swings over and *crack*! The lobster damages the crab's claw.

The lobster grabs a couple of legs. Now the crab can't run away. The lobster and the crab fight back and forth. The crab's claws are not strong enough to hurt the lobster.

The lobster moves its crusher claw and bites a chunk off the crab's face.

The crab fills with water from the hole in its shell. This is fatal. The crab slowly stops moving.

The lobster agrees with people. Crabs are delicious.

RATTLESNAKE VS. SECRETARY BIRD

The rattlesnake is hungry and is looking for a bird to eat. What bird should it go after? If it attacks a bird, who would win?

BIRDS OF PREY

Should the rattlesnake attack an osprey? This ocean bird eats by catching fish with its sharp talons.

NAME FACT
Ospreys are also called sea hawks.

A bald eagle? It is a national symbol of the United States of America.

FACT
You can find it on a one-dollar bill.

A barn owl? It eats mice, voles, shrews, and other small mammals.

STEALTH FACT
An owl's feathers are shaped so it can fly quietly.

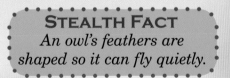

A vulture? Not a pretty bird. It eats carrion.

DEFINITION
Carrion is the rotten body of a dead animal.

OTHER BIRDS

A peacock? What beautiful tail feathers! This bird is in the pheasant family.

A wild turkey? Sorry, turkey!

A sandhill crane? It looks like a dinosaur with feathers.

SOUND FACT
Sandhill cranes squawk so loud you can hear them miles away.

A hummingbird? No! Too small!

SIZE FACT
A hummingbird egg is the size of an M&M.

None of these birds look interesting enough! How about a secretary bird? What a strange name. We'll meet it soon.

MEET THE RATTLESNAKE

The western diamondback rattlesnake is a venomous snake found in North America. Its scientific name is *Crotalus atrox*. Its name means "fierce rattle."

NAME FACT
Repeated sheddings of its skin creates a rattle at the end of its tail. When threatened, this snake rattles its tail.

DANGER
Venomous means having a poisonous bite.

You can identify different rattlesnakes by the designs on their scales. Do you see the diamond skin pattern?

The secretary bird lives in Africa. Its scientific name is *Sagittarius serpentarius*. It has an unusual diet—it eats snakes and other animals.

STARRY NAME
Its scientific name comes from two constellations: Sagittarius, *which means archer, and* serpentarius, *which means serpent handler.*

FACT
Birds don't have arms and hands; they have wings.

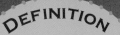

DEFINITION
A constellation is a pattern of stars in the sky that makes a shape.

Its head looks like it is surrounded by quill pens. That's how it got the name secretary bird.

LENGTH

The western diamondback rattlesnake can grow up to about 7 feet long. Here are silhouettes of a basketball player and a rattlesnake.

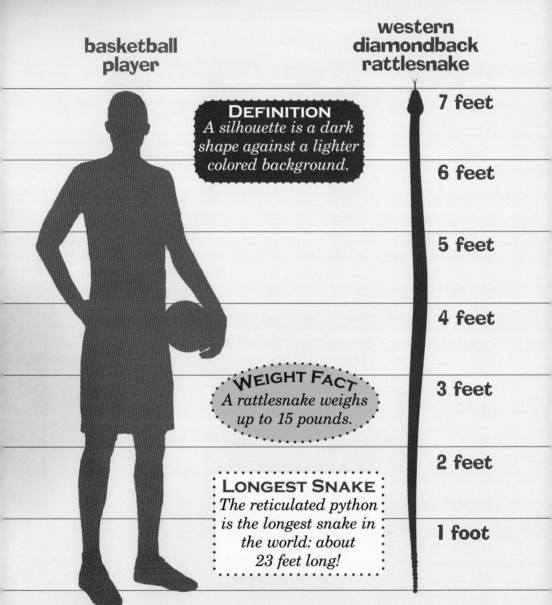

basketball player

western diamondback rattlesnake

DEFINITION
A silhouette is a dark shape against a lighter colored background.

7 feet

6 feet

5 feet

4 feet

WEIGHT FACT
A rattlesnake weighs up to 15 pounds.

3 feet

2 feet

LONGEST SNAKE
The reticulated python is the longest snake in the world: about 23 feet long!

1 foot

If you hear the rattle, stay away! It's not the biggest or the smallest snake. But it is a deadly, venomous snake.

HEIGHT

For a bird, it's really tall. A secretary bird can grow up to 4 feet high. That's taller than most kindergartners.

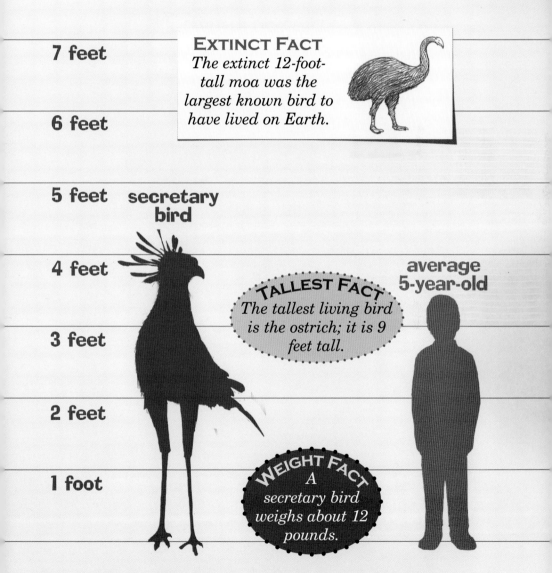

7 feet

EXTINCT FACT
The extinct 12-foot-tall moa was the largest known bird to have lived on Earth.

6 feet

5 feet secretary bird

4 feet

average 5-year-old

TALLEST FACT
The tallest living bird is the ostrich; it is 9 feet tall.

3 feet

2 feet

WEIGHT FACT
A secretary bird weighs about 12 pounds.

1 foot

Most of its height is in its legs. Long, skinny legs!

IT'S A REPTILE

A reptile is a cold-blooded vertebrate animal that is covered in dry scales or horny plates. Snakes, lizards, crocodilians, and turtles are reptiles.

DID YOU KNOW?
Vertebrate means an animal with a spinal cord.

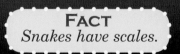

FACT
Most reptiles lay eggs.

FACT
Snakes have scales.

The rattlesnake has a forked tongue. Its tongue is multitalented; it can taste, smell, and tell temperature.

IT'S A BIRD

Birds are warm-blooded, winged vertebrates that are covered in feathers, and have scaly legs, and a beak.

GROUNDED FACT
Kiwis, penguins, kakapos, chickens, ostriches, emus, cassowaries, elephant birds, and rheas cannot fly.

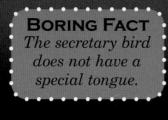

BORING FACT
The secretary bird does not have a special tongue.

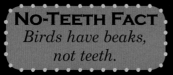

NO-TEETH FACT
Birds have beaks, not teeth.

RATTLESNAKE SKELETON

This is a rattlesnake skeleton. Ribs, ribs, and more ribs!
What does the skeleton remind you of?

a. coiled spring
b. Slinky
c. dragon
d. all of the above

NUMBER FACT
Humans have 33 vertebrae
and 12 sets of ribs.

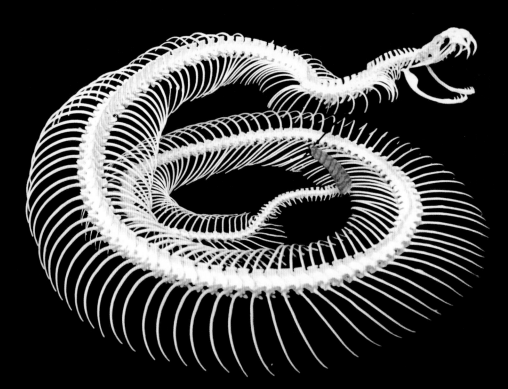

ANOTHER NUMBER
Rattlesnakes have between 200 and
400 vertebrae and ribs!

FACT
Snakes have teeth
called fangs.

SECRETARY BIRD SKELETON

This is the skeleton of a secretary bird. What does it remind you of? Does it look like a dinosaur skeleton?

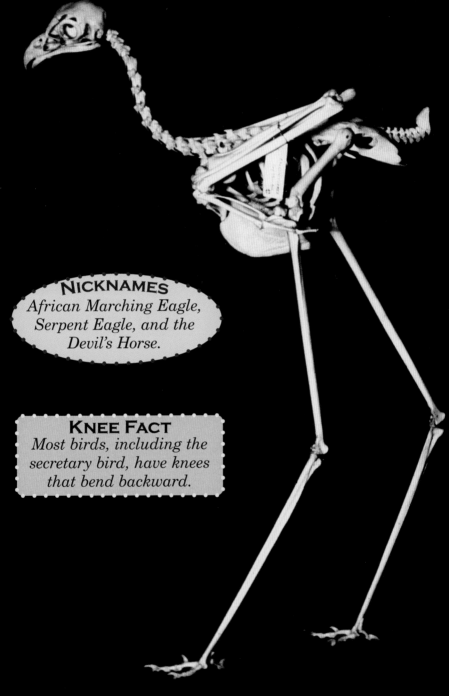

NICKNAMES
African Marching Eagle, Serpent Eagle, and the Devil's Horse.

KNEE FACT
Most birds, including the secretary bird, have knees that bend backward.

FIND ME

Western diamondback rattlesnakes live mostly in western North America. Here is where they live.

UNITED STATES

MEXICO

western diamondback territory

CONTEST FACT
When people have a contest to catch rattlesnakes, it is called a rattlesnake roundup.

WORLD MAP

LOOK FOR ME

The secretary bird lives in the grassy plains and savannahs of Africa.

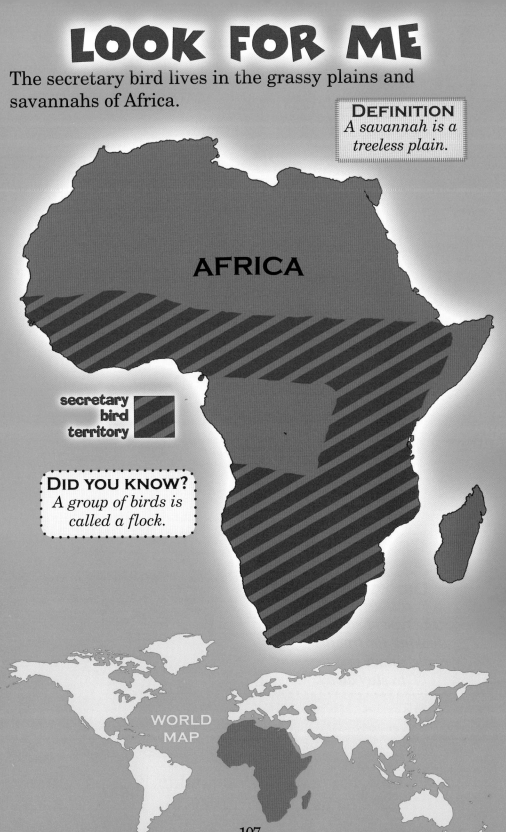

AFRICA

secretary
bird
territory

DID YOU KNOW?
A group of birds is called a flock.

WORLD
MAP

WHAT'S SPECIAL?

What is special about rattlesnakes? Rattles!

Rattlesnakes molt and shed their skin. The more times
they shed, the longer their rattles.

WHAT'S UNIQUE?

What is special about secretary birds? They have the longest legs of any bird of prey. Their lower legs are extra skinny. This protects the secretary bird, because there is nothing there for a snake to bite.

Their toes are as sharp as razor blades. Watch out—they kick, they stomp! They even kick snakes.

DELICIOUS

Rattlesnakes prefer to eat small mammals. This rattlesnake is eating a mouse.

Rattlesnakes eat rabbits, rats, voles, mice, squirrels, gerbils, prairie dogs, chipmunks, and hamsters.

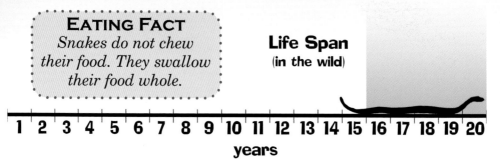

EATING FACT
Snakes do not chew their food. They swallow their food whole.

Life Span
(in the wild)

1 2 3 4 5 6 7 8 9 10 11 12 13 14 15 16 17 18 19 20
years

Rattlesnakes have no interest in eating humans. People are too big for them. Rattlesnakes eat only what they can swallow whole. They also eat frogs, birds, lizards, and other snakes.

YUMMY

The secretary bird eats snakes and lizards. When they find snakes, they kick them with their razor-sharp claws. Whap! Whap! Whap! They also attack with their sharp beaks.

Here is a secretary bird eating a lizard. It looks delicious! Can you imagine eating a live lizard?

Life Span
(in the wild)

1 2 3 4 5 6 7 8 9 10 11 12 13 14 15 16 17 18 19 20
years

YOUNG FACT
Young secretary birds eat insects.

PLUMAGE
The arrangement, color, and shape of a bird's feathers is called its plumage.

FAMOUS

There is a Major League Baseball team called the Arizona Diamondbacks.

The Florida A&M Rattlers have a great logo on their helmet.

ODDBALL

Secretary bird is a strange name. Should it be renamed the soccer bird because of its kicking ability?

I can head the ball, too.

STRANGE
It is a unique bird. It has a face like an eagle, legs like a stork, and it eats like a bird of prey.

The secretary bird is the national symbol of Sudan. It's also on the coat of arms of South Africa.

SUDAN

SOUTH AFRICA

SLOW

Rattlesnakes move slowly. They slither up to 2 or 3 miles per hour.

SAFE FACT
Rattlesnakes can go underground to hide and be safe. Their home is called a den.

FUN FACT
A den is the home of a community of snakes. A burrow is the home of one snake.

HIDE LOW

DID YOU KNOW?
Up to 200 rattlesnakes can live in one den.

RUN

The secretary bird runs fast. It is considered a terrestrial bird. That means it mostly stays on the ground. It prefers to run.

SPEED LIMIT 20

SLEEP HIGH

At night, secretary birds fly high up in acacia trees and safely sleep. Lions, hyenas, and jackals can't get them in a tree.

WEAPONS

Rattlesnakes have fangs and poisonous venom. They bite and then inject the venom through the hollow fangs.

FACT
Rattlesnake venom is a coagulant. It ruins the lining of your cells.

When it attacks, it is lightning fast.

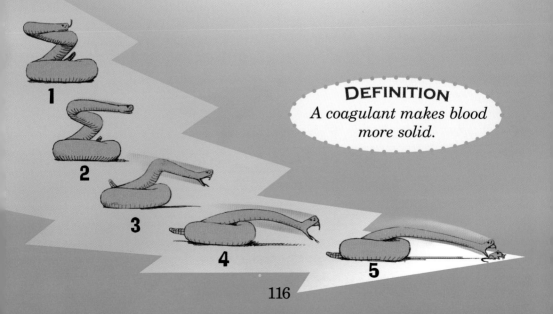

DEFINITION
A coagulant makes blood more solid.

1
2
3
4
5

WEAPONS

The secretary bird has four great weapons. It can fly, run fast, and has a sharp beak and deadly claws.

> ### DEFINITION
> *A raptor is a bird that hunts and eats other animals.*

It can jab with its beak, stomp with its feet, and kick with its long legs.

The secretary bird is in an acacia tree, ready to hunt. It's on the lookout. In the wild, it is eat or be eaten. The secretary bird looks down on the ground for food.

The rattlesnake is safe and sound in its den. It's getting hungry. It decides to take a peek outside.

The rattlesnake sticks its head out of its hole. It's looking for a tasty mouse or a delicious rat to eat. The secretary bird sees the snake, swoops down, and uses its feet to stomp the rattlesnake's head.

Ouch, that hurt! The snake wiggles back into its den.

Now the secretary bird is on the ground. It can fly, but it can also run fast. It looks around. Where did that snake go? The snake decides to fake out the bird and use its secret second escape tunnel.

The bird hears it. As the rattlesnake moves out of the den, the secretary bird uses its foot to stomp on the snake again.

The snake moves into a defensive position to bite the bird. The secretary bird's body is too tall for the snake to reach. The snake tries to sink its fangs into the bird's ankle. But there isn't enough there to bite. The bird dances away.

The snake tries to bite again. Yikes! Poison! The bird has to be careful. The bird kicks the snake. Whap! Then the bird stomps on the snake with its razor-sharp claws.

Whap! The bird kicks the snake again. The snake goes flying in the air.

The snake lands on the ground. It decides to skip dinner and escape to its den.

As the snake moves back and forth across the ground, the secretary bird keeps on kicking it. Whap! Whap! Whap! In between kicks, the secretary bird pecks the snake on its head. Bop! The rattlesnake is wounded.

BALANCE FACT

The secretary bird uses its wings to balance itself while stomping on a snake.

The bird gives it another kick! Whap!

The secretary bird eats the rattlesnake. The fight is over. What must it be like to eat a wounded venomous snake? Yuck!

WHO HAS THE ADVANTAGE? CHECKLIST

GREEN ANTS		ARMY ANTS
☐	JAWS	☐
☐	ACID SPRAY	☐
☐	STINGER	☐
☐	NUMBERS	☐
☐	SPEED	☐
☐	WEIGHT	☐
☐	CAMOUFLAGE	☐

If you were the author, how would you rewrite the ending?

WHO HAS THE ADVANTAGE? CHECKLIST

JAGUAR   SKUNK

JAGUAR		SKUNK
☐	Size	☐
☐	Teeth	☐
☐	Stink	☐
☐	Claws	☐
☐	Speed	☐
☐	Weight	☐

Author's note: Maybe you can write your own
Who Would Win? book. Who do you think a jaguar
should fight?

WHO HAS THE ADVANTAGE?
CHECKLIST

LOBSTER   **BLUE CRAB**

LOBSTER		BLUE CRAB
☐	Size	☐
☐	Shell	☐
☐	Claws	☐
☐	Legs	☐
☐	Teeth	☐
☐	Speed	☐
☐	Tail	☐

Author note: This is one way the fight might have ended.
How would you write the ending?

WHO HAS THE ADVANTAGE? CHECKLIST

RATTLESNAKE   ## SECRETARY BIRD

RATTLESNAKE		SECRETARY BIRD
☐	Size	☐
☐	Venom	☐
☐	Claws	☐
☐	Legs	☐
☐	Flight	☐
☐	Speed	☐
☐	Tail	☐

Author's note: This is one way the fight might have ended. How would you write the ending?

WILD
WARRIORS